LOS ANGELES
LAKERS

LOS ANGELES
LAKERS

ANN SCHWAB

CREATIVE EDUCATION

Photo Credit: Creative Education would like to thank NBA photographer Ron Koch (New York City) for the color photography in this series.

Published by Creative Education Inc., 123 South Broad Street, Mankato, Minnesota 56001.

ISBN: 0-88682-208-4

Los Angeles, California, is without question one of the world's top entertainment capitals. It is home to many famous movie stars, television personalities and recording artists. But some of the city's most popular entertainers wear the uniform of the Los Angeles Lakers pro basketball team.

If you're a Laker fan, you already know that players such as Kareem Abdul-Jabbar, Magic Johnson, James Worthy, Mychal Thompson, Byron Scott, Michael Cooper and A.C. Green are just the latest in a long line of Laker superstars who have lit up the NBA over the past four decades. In fact, next to the Boston Celtics, the Lakers have had the most star-studded and successful history in professional basketball.

The Lakers' story begins several decades ago, before the birth of the NBA. The franchise was formed in the 1940s as part of the Basketball Association of America. At that time, the BAA was just one of several pro leagues that was struggling to lure American football and baseball fans over to basketball. The Lakers represented Minneapolis, Minnesota, the Land of 10,000 Lakes, a fact which explains how the team got its name.

By 1950, the BAA had merged with the National Basketball League to form the National Basketball Association. Over the next five years, many of the league's charter members would fall by the wayside, but the Lakers were an instant success.

The league's first superstar, George Mikan, was the heart and soul of the Lakers. The sportswriters of the time were so dazzled by his talent and power that they reverently referred to Mikan as "Mr. Basketball" or "The Ace." Though George's choirboy smile and wire-rimmed spectacles made him appear gentle and studious off the court, he was a terror on the basketball floor.

Earvin "Magic" Johnson led the Lakers to five NBA titles in the 1980s.

At 6-foot-10, 245 pounds, Mikan towered over most of the centers of that era. He was so dominant that the NBA had to change the rules just to keep him from totally overpowering the other teams. For example, the three-second lane was widened from 6 feet to 12 feet in the early 1950s just so Mikan couldn't stand by the basket and slam dunk the ball all night. But the new rule didn't slow him down much. The nimble giant continued to work his way inside, control the boards and toss in sweeping left-handed hook shots from the top of the key.

George was such a great player that the reader-board announcing an upcoming game at Madison Square Garden once carried the message: Tonight George Mikan vs. New York Knicks.

With Mikan in the middle, the Minneapolis Lakers became the NBA's first dynasty. For the first half of the 1950s, they were almost un-beatable. Not only did they win the world championship in their charter season, but they took three more straight titles from 1952-54.

After the Lakers' initial success, two events combined to bring an end to their league domina-tion. First, George Mikan retired after the 1954 season. Next, coach Red Auerbach of the Boston Celtics pulled off a blockbuster trade that landed the one-and-only Bill Russell in Boston. Sudden-ly, the balance of power had shifted. The Lakers dynasty was coming to a close.

Legendary George Mikan lofts one over Nat "Sweetwater" Clifton in the fourth game of the 1953 NBA title series.

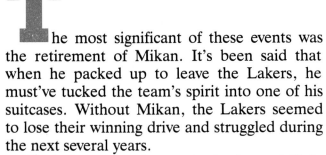

The most significant of these events was the retirement of Mikan. It's been said that when he packed up to leave the Lakers, he must've tucked the team's spirit into one of his suitcases. Without Mikan, the Lakers seemed to lose their winning drive and struggled during the next several years.

But help was on the way in the form of Elgin Baylor, a cat quick, 6-foot-5 forward from Seattle University. "Elgin was a cut above the rest," explained sportswriter Jim Moore. "He combined terrific court savvy with tremendous body control and some of the best inside moves ever seen in the league. Now add the fact that Baylor almost never missed from inside 20 feet, even when shooting off-balance or from odd angles, and it's clear why he was considered one of the best players of his era."

Right from the beginning, Baylor injected new spirit into the Laker lineup. He put lots of points on the board and inspired his teammates to new heights. Suddenly, the Lakers were an explosive team again. Their new-found shooting power was enough to demoralize every team in the league. Every team, that is, except the Celtics.

"Hot Rod" Hundley

. . . the Lakers made it all the way to the championship series that year . . .

Consider, for example, the Laker-Celtic game of February 27, 1959. With Baylor leading all Lakers in scoring, Minneapolis reeled off 139 points against Boston. Unfortunately for the Lakers, the Celtic lineup scored a breathtaking 173 points.

Despite this setback, the Lakers made it all the way to the championship series that year, only to be swept in four games by archrival Boston. Baylor finished the season as the NBA's fourth-leading scorer, made the All-NBA team, was named Rookie of the Year and was the co-MVP of the All-Star game.

Elgin Baylor

Even with the excitement of the Laker-Celtic rivalry, attendance was low in Minneapolis. At the end of the 1959-60 season, the decision was made to move the team to Los Angeles. Fans throughout the country were saddened to see a team with such a great tradition uprooted from its original home. But the NBA welcomed the opportunity to establish a new team on the West Coast.

So, off went the Lakers to the city of bright lights, night life and movie stars. Lakers head coach Fred Schaus later recalled that all but one of the players adjusted easily to the new surroundings. The one who didn't was Jerry West, a clean-cut young rookie who looked as if he had just fallen off a Wheaties boxcover.

"Jerry was this small-town guy from West Virginia," coach Schaus commented. "For awhile, he seemed in awe of the city and the veteran NBA players who had

He is the greatest pure shooter the game has ever known . . . he is the man who has everything.

been his idols in college. Once he got over the jitters, though, he quickly became one of the all-time greats.

"He is the greatest pure shooter the game has ever known," Schaus continued. "If you sat down to build a perfect 6-foot-3 basketball player, you would come up with Jerry West. He is the man who has everything: fine shooting touch, speed, quickness, all the physical assets and a tremendous dedication to the game."

The great Jerry West (44) streaks for a loose ball in a 1969 match-up against the Baltimore Bullets at the Forum.

West averaged nearly 20 points a game during his rookie season, but he was more than just a scoring guard. He became a playmaker of the highest order, helping Elgin Baylor, Ray Felix, Tom Hawking, Rod Hundley and the rest of the team perform exceptional feats. On November 15, 1960, Elgin Baylor received nationwide acclaim for setting a new NBA record of 71 points against the New York Knicks. But much of the credit rightfully belonged to West, whose remarkable passing had made it all possible.

Thanks primarily to Baylor and West, the Lakers finished second in the Western Conference in 1961, and then won Western Division championships or playoff spots in 1962 through 1968. Despite the team's success, the Boston Celtics won the NBA championship year after year. No matter how well the Lakers played, the Celtics always seemed to play a little bit better when it counted the most.

As the years wore on, the fans in Los Angeles spoke ominously of the Boston jinx. It was said that frustration was spelled B-O-S-T-O-N in Los Angeles. After all, the Lakers hadn't won a title since the days of George Mikan.

Convinced that the team needed a center as dominant as Mikan to capture the league championship, the Lakers stunned the NBA by acquiring superstar Wilt Chamberlain from Philadelphia in 1968.

Nimble giant: Towering Wilt Chamberlain moves like a cat-quick guard in this drive for two around Chicago's Jim Fox. (1971)

Chamberlain, coming off two consecutive MVP seasons, was considered basketball's greatest offensive player. In his nine years in the NBA, he had already scored over 25,000 points and had played in the All-Star Game each season. One year, Wilt averaged an incredible 50 points and 25 rebounds a game. In 1962, he shattered Baylor's record by pumping in 100 points in a single game against New York.

Now the Lakers had a triple threat in Elgin Baylor, Jerry West and Chamberlain. Could a world championship be far behind?

It looked as though the 1968-69 season would be their year. Chamberlain led the league in rebounds and field goal percentage as Los Angeles finished first in their conference. The Lakers marched all the way to the championship series only to have Wilt pull up lame in the final period of the seventh and deciding game. The result

was another championship for Boston, their eleventh in thirteen seasons.

After several more disappointing years, the 1972 season brought an end to the frustration for the Lakers. Despite the retirement of Elgin Baylor, the club went on to record the winningest season of any team in NBA history. They won an astounding 69 regular season games, including a breathtaking streak of 33 straight.

It was a team effort all the way. Gail Goodrich averaged 25.9 points, Jerry West dished out a league-leading 747 assists, and Jim McMillian and Happy Hairston sizzled on the front line. Meanwhile, Chamberlain was pure magic. A typical game saw Wilt score 31 points and snag 16 rebounds.

In the playoffs, the Lakers rolled past Chicago and Milwaukee to meet the New York Knicks for the NBA title. Playing with a sprained wrist during the championship game, Chamberlain dominated, scoring 24 points and grabbing 29 rebounds. It was the eighth time in eleven years that the team had reached the final round of the playoffs. But it was the first time the Lakers were victorious.

After several more successful years, an era came to a close for the Lakers with the retirement of Jerry West and Wilt Chamberlain in the mid-1970s. Without them, the Lakers would have a hard time regaining their championship form. But, as always, they wouldn't be down long.

. . . the club went on to record the winningest season of any team in NBA history. They won an astounding 69 regular season games.

The Lakers thought it would be next to impossible to replace Chamberlain. But that was before they met the extraordinary Kareem Abdul-Jabbar. When the Lakers acquired the quiet, graceful center from Milwaukee in 1975, Jabbar had already become one of the most renowned players in NBA history.

As a first-year player out of UCLA, he had won NBA Rookie of the Year honors by averaging 28.8 points, pulling down 1,190 rebounds, dishing out 337 assists and playing superior defense. During Kareem's stint with Milwaukee, the Bucks had gone on to win one league championship, and Jabbar had garnered three MVP awards.

One of the largest players in the NBA at 7-foot-2 and 267 pounds, Jabbar's size had always been impressive. At birth he measured 22.5 inches and weighed 12 pounds. By the age of ten, he stood over 6 feet tall.

Kareem's talent grew to match his stature. As an eighth grader he could already slam dunk with ease. At New York City's Power Memorial High School, Jabbar earned national recognition by scoring over 2,000 points as he led his teams to a 95-6 record and three state championships over four years. He continued to dominate on the collegiate level. At UCLA, he took the Bruins to three consecutive NCAA titles and was named collegiate player of the year twice.

Head and shoulders above the best in the league: Kareem's career with the Lakers spans two decades and five world championships.

In his first season with the Lakers, Jabbar earned his fourth MVP award. He led the league in rebounds, blocked shots and minutes played. At times, he single-handedly dominated entire teams with his patented skyhook, a shot perfected years before on the streets of New York City.

"Bringing in Kareem is like wheeling out nuclear weapons," said rival coach Del Harris. Certainly, the future looked rosy for the Lakers.

But even though the Lakers gained playoff berths each season under the leadership of Jerry West, who rejoined the team as head coach in 1976, they had little success in post-season play. The team was loaded with talent but seemed to lack a certain spark.

The remedy for the Lakers' listless play proved to be Earvin "Magic" Johnson. When Magic joined the club in 1979, he became the sparkplug that finally ignited the explosive Laker scoring machine of the 1980s. Even as a

He single-handedly dominated entire teams with his patented skyhook . . .

Earvin "Magic" Johnson

rookie, Magic's engaging personality showed through. He combined the ballhandling of Walt Frazier with the coolness of Earl Monroe and the showmanship of Meadowlark Lemon.

"Summer was all basketball for me," Magic said of his youth. "Me and my friends would get up real early and play hoops all morning 'til it got too hot. When it cooled off a little, we'd go back and play HORSE or one-on-one until dark."

By the time he entered high school, Earvin's skills had developed far beyond his years. He earned the nickname "Magic" following a 36 point, 18 rebound and 16 assist performance.

In Magic's freshman year of college at Michigan State, he led the Spartans to their first Big Ten title in 19 years. They followed that up with an NCAA title the next season. In the championship game, Magic out-dueled Indiana's Larry Bird, the future Boston Celtics star, and was named the Final Four MVP. Not surprisingly, the Lakers selected Magic as the number one pick in the college draft following his sophomore year.

With Magic strutting his stuff, the Lakers returned to greatness in 1979-80. Jack McKinney coached the team for the first 13 games before being injured in a freak

Norm Nixon

bicycle accident. Paul Westhead took over as head coach, and Pat Riley was lured from his job in the Lakers' broadcast booth to become assistant coach.

Westhead's Lakers sported a hard-running fast-break attack, and most teams withered under the pressure. After completing a successful regular season, the Lakers easily defeated Seattle and Phoenix in the playoffs to advance to the NBA Finals where they faced the powerful Philadelphia 76ers.

The Lakers took three of the first five games in the championship series. But their fans sensed doom when Jabbar was sidelined with an injured foot late in Game 5. That meant that the Lakers would have to play Game 6 at Philadelphia's home court without their superstar center. Surely, the Sixers would win and tie the series.

But no. With Kareem rooting from the sidelines, 20-year-old Magic Johnson exploded for 42 points, 15 rebounds and 7 assists as the Lakers romped to the title. Johnson became the first rookie ever to be named Most Valuable Player in the championship playoffs. Handing the trophy to Kareem, Magic reminded the reporters, "If it weren't for the big fella we wouldn't even be here."

The Lakers would have to play Game 6 at Philadelphia's home court without their superstar center. Surely the Sixers would win . . .

One of the best-loved and highest paid athletes in the world of sport, Magic Johnson is often referred to as the "heartbeat of the Lakers."

With this victory, the Lakers began a decade of league dominance that would rival the success enjoyed by the Boston Celtics during the 1960s. Los Angeles became the premier team of the NBA, making seven appearances in the championship series during the 1980s. They emerged as NBA champs five times, including back-to-back championships in 1987 and 1988. It was the first time in 19 years that any team won consecutive NBA titles, a feat last accomplished by the 1968-69 Celtics.

One change in the Laker organization was instrumental to the team's incredible success. After a dismal start to the 1982 season, owner Jerry Buss felt the Lakers were simply not living up to their potential. Paul Westhead was asked to step aside, and assistant Pat Riley took over as head coach.

Under Riley, the Lakers exploded for 11 victories in 13 games and never looked back. They went on to win 50 of

---

Just like that, Riley had a world title in his first year as head coach.

---

their final 71 games, then breezed through the playoffs winning 12 of 14 contests, including an NBA record nine wins in a row. Just like that, Riley had a world title in his first year as head coach. Basketball fans throughout the nation wondered "Who is this guy?"

■

Coach Pat Riley (right), shown here with San Antonio Spurs coach Stan Albeck, led the Lakers to dynasty status during the 1980s.

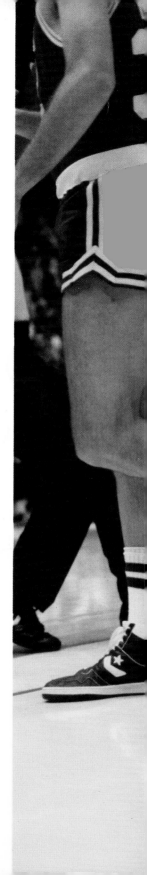

Long-time Laker fans knew the answer to that question. Ten years earlier those fans had watched Riley play his heart out as a member of the record-setting Laker team that had won 69 games and the NBA title in 1972. Then during the late 1970s, the fans had tuned in as Riley called the action during his three-year stint as the Lakers' color commentator.

"Laker blood flows through Riley's veins," said owner Jerry Buss. "He was on a Laker team once that won 33 in a row, but that's not what you hear him talk about. Riley thinks and talks about the Lakers of today and tomorrow. He has a bright, clear vision for our team, and the players respond to it."

When Riley took command of the Lakers, the club was built around Kareem Abdul-Jabbar and Magic Johnson. Their supporting cast was comprised of Norm Nixon, Jamaal Wilkes, Bob McAdoo and Kurt Rambis. While these players had just delivered the NBA championship, Riley, with an eye to the future, began a subtle rebuilding program.

Magic and Kareem remained the cornerstone of the Lakers, but the rest of the key players changed to include James Worthy, Byron Scott, A.C. Greene, Michael Cooper and Mychal Thompson. It is a testament to Riley's coaching genius that he was able to maintain the championship caliber of his club while it underwent such a drastic personnel shift.

Rugged, hard working Kurt Rambis came to the Lakers as a free agent in 1981 and quickly became a fan favorite.

ne of Riley's first moves was to work Michael Cooper, a 1978 draft pick, into the lineup. Cooper, a 6-foot-7, 176 pound guard/forward, had been an All-American at New Mexico University. Once in the Laker lineup, he quickly blossomed into one of the league's top defenders. In 1986, he would become the NBA's Defensive Player of the Year.

In 1982, Riley used his first college draft as head coach to further bolster his front court. The Lakers had the number one pick in the draft and they used it to select James Worthy, a 6-foot-9, 225-pound forward out of North Carolina. Worthy had just led the Tar Heels to the 1982 NCAA championship with a one point victory over Georgetown. He was named Final Four MVP following a game-high 28 point performance in the collegiate title game.

Worthy quickly became a vital ingredient in the Lakers' success. In his first year with the club, he was a unanimous choice for the league's All-Rookie team, scoring over 1,000 points during the season.

Rickey Green of the Utah Jazz faces double trouble from Lakers James Worthy (42) and Norm Nixon in 1982 action at the Forum.

Having established Cooper and Worthy in the front court, Riley now turned his attention to the back court. Looking for a young player with scoring punch, the Lakers traded Norm Nixon for rookie Byron Scott in 1983. Although he played just three years at Arizona State University, Scott left the school as its all-time scoring leader. With the Lakers, he became one of the NBA's best shooting guards and in 1987-88 led the Lakers with a 21.7 scoring average.

The next key acquisition was A.C. Greene, a 6-foot-9, 224-pound forward, and an All-American at Oregon State University. Selected in the first round of the 1985 draft by Los Angeles, Greene soon became an integral part of the Lakers defense.

Riley also strengthened his bench considerably with the addition of Mychal Thompson, a fierce competitor skilled in both offense and defense. Thompson, a six-year

Riley . . . guaranteed that his team would repeat as world champions the following year.

NBA veteran, was acquired by the Lakers in a February, 1987 trade with the San Antonio Spurs.

With this solid core of players, the Lakers went on to become league champions in 1985, 1987 and 1988. After the Lakers had clinched the 1987 NBA title, Riley, an expert motivator, publicly guaranteed that his team would repeat as world champions the following year.

To bolster the Lakers' back court scoring punch, Coach Riley snagged deadeye Byron Scott from the Clippers' trading block in 1983.

Riley's bold prediction laid the framework for the 1987-88 season. "Guaranteeing a championship was the best thing Pat ever did," said Byron Scott. "It set the stage in our mind. Work harder, be better. That's the only way we could repeat."

Even though the Lakers posted the best record in the NBA, they endured a grueling 24-game playoff season. The young Detroit Pistons, with their physical play and sparkling defense, took the Lakers down to the wire in the championship series.

But in the end, the Lakers prevailed. Riley's promise was fulfilled. James Worthy was named series MVP as he recorded the first triple double of his career in the title game with 36 points, 16 rebounds and 10 assists.

While the Lakers were the NBA's preeminent team of the 1980s, more challenges lay just ahead. With the emergence of new league powers, the Lakers will face strong rivals in the years to come. But with their winning style, the Los Angeles Lakers will surely remain title contenders for years to come. ■

DATE DUE

Metro Litho
Oak Forest, IL 60452

11	5	13	
10	16	8	
12	14	14	
12	11	8	
16	12	4	
11	7	5	
11	16	14	
11	13		
	8		

94471

796.32   Schwab, Ann
Sch   Los Angeles Lakers